What This Book Will Do for You

By the end of this book, you will have a deeper understanding of what it means to be a better first-time manager and be able to create an environment in which you and other people can all meet your own needs, wishes, and goals by using effective methods for dealing with people, for interviewing and hiring, for problem solving and decision making, for reviewing and appraising work. So read on . . .

Other Titles in the Successful Office Skills Series

HOW TO BE A
Successful
MANAGER

Donald H. Weiss

amacom
American Management Association

This book is available at a special
discount when ordered in bulk quantities.
For information, contact Special Sales Department,
AMACOM, a division of American Management Association,
135 West 50th Street, New York, NY 10020.

Library of Congress Cataloging-in-Publication Data

Weiss, Donald H., 1936-
    How to be a successful manager.

    (The Successful office skills series)
    Bibliography: p.
    Includes index.
    1. Executive ability. I. Title. II. Series.
HD38.2.W45   1986   658.4'09   85-26836
ISBN 0-8144-7642-2

Printing number

10 9 8 7 6 5 4 3

CONTENTS

Contents

Introduction—
Becoming a Manager

Starting a new job—any new job—is tough enough. But when you take on a new job in the place where you've been working for several years, and that new job results from a promotion into management, that makes the new job even tougher. It seems that everyone in the place has an eye on you. Your boss, your boss's boss, and worst of all, your co-workers. In your mind, you feel a kinship with a chimpanzee at the zoo—on display for all the world to see everything you do.

The world Dolores O'Shea confronted that early summer Monday morning seemed a lot like that. Newly promoted by United Property and Casualty Insurance to be supervisor of auto claims, she drove slowly into the parking lot of the steel and glass tower overlooking the bay. The rising sun gleamed brightly off the face of the building as she pressed her shiny plastic card into the meter at the gate. While she waited for the arm to lift, she noted, for no apparent reason, that by the time she left that day, the sun would be on the other side of the building.

And where would Dolores O'Shea be on the next morning? Would she be coming back in this gate, shielding her eyes from the bright morning sun? With a humorless, almost grim chuckle, she spoke out loud to herself. "Yesterday I couldn't spell *supervisor*. Today I am one."

She had been promoted to take charge of five highly trained, well-qualified adjusters who had vied and jockied for a crack at this position. She got it because, while

1

they were each excellent technicians, they were none of them supervisory material. They lacked the people skills required of a supervisor. They lacked the personal discipline to organize their own work properly, let alone the work of other people. The good part was that none of them seemed to resent the decision to promote Dolores. They, too, knew that, of them all, she was the best suited for the job.

As she walked slowly through the parking lot to the main entrance, Dolores reviewed the plan she had pulled together over the weekend. Though the company doesn't have a supervisory-skills training program, her boss, John, gave her some help. Still, she was essentially on her own—too visible to escape everyone's notice and too vulnerable unless she took steps of her own.

Well, Dolores thought, I'm a good adjuster, and I know the people in the unit. Good people—Bob Levitt and Mary Powell, two 8-year veterans; Janet Jones, Phyllis Jackson, and Allen Adams, with 17 years experience between them. All that training, experience, and savvy had turned the department into an efficient machine. And she was authorized to hire two additional people, one to replace her and one to round out the growing unit. All it would take to make it into an effective organization would be to get everyone working together as a cooperative team. That, Dolores realized, was to be her responsibility.

Dolores entered the building, her head high, her jaw set firmly. This was it. After ten years as an all-lines adjuster, she was finally moving up—and nothing would get her to blow this chance.

What Is a Manager?

Dolores confronts challenges that to one degree or another you may face yourself—right now—even if you're not in a supervisory position yet. Although she was joking about not knowing how to spell *supervisor,* that insecurity about what one is doing is all too common. Many people are promoted into managerial positions without having had any experience and/or training in the duties they're expected to perform. Good technicians, such as Dolores, good salespeople, people who have excelled at one type of job—all are promoted, with little or no preparation, into a completely different, difficult position of authority. Oh, they probably know how to spell the word *supervisor,* but most of them would be hard-pressed to define it or to describe what a supervisor does.

As in the case of any organized activity, becoming an effective supervisor requires a coherent strategy. In order to help you plan the proper strategy, I'm going to take a tack very different from what you might expect. Though I'll define the supervisor's job, describe its functions, I'll do so by looking at the main objective any manager has, whether it be a first-line, middle-level, or executive position. Then, I'll describe the functions of management: handling people, hiring, problem solving and decision making, monitoring and reviewing work, and conducting appraisals.

What Does a Manager Do?

When John told Dolores of her promotion, they talked for a bit, and he said something that makes sense for any new supervisor to learn.

Dolores: You know how much I want this promotion, but I really am a bit frightened of it.
John: What's frightening you?
Dolores: Bottom line? I don't think I know what's expected of me.

John: We have a lot of confidence in you, Dolores.

Dolores: I guess I'm the only one around here who doesn't, John. I'm a good adjuster, but I've never had any experience as a supervisor. We have no supervisory-skills classes here, either. I guess I'll have to go to night school.

John: That's a good idea; but Dolores, I want you to keep one thing in mind. It's something a manager of mine once told me. A manager has one and only one responsibility—to get the right results by the proper use of your resources. You're bright, you're creative. You get along with people well. You've already demonstrated leadership capabilities. I have no doubts about you at all.

The important advice? *A manager has one and only one mandate—to achieve the results required of him or her during any given period of time through the effective utilization of the resources at his or her disposal.*

That's neither a definition nor a description. It's a goal, the anatomy of which consists of a target (to get results of some specific nature), a deadline (a given period of time), and a set of conditions (the effective utilization of resources). Dolores now knows that her performance will be judged by how well she achieves this goal.

Results vary with the type of unit or department you manage. In the case of an insurance-claims unit, results could consist of the number of claim files closed in the given time period, the total dollars in settlements meted out, the reduction in costs of operations over a comparable period, and so on. In another kind of unit,

4

the amount of income generated may be the result required. In still another, it could be the number of units of product completed. The mission of the company and the mission of your unit prescribe the results you're expected to achieve.

That's what it boils down to: the results *you're* expected to achieve. As a supervisor, you have people (one of your resources) through whom you will try to get the work done. Yet when it comes down to the so-called bottom line, whether or not the goal is reached remains your responsibility. You're responsible for whether or not the people get that work done and for how well they do it. That's why Dolores mentally inventoried the experience and training of the people she has working for her and why she accepted for herself the responsibility for melding those people into an effective work group.

When it comes to utilizing resources, you can look at them in two ways: first, material resources; second, human resources. There's a ratio between the cost of those resources and the benefit, or return, to be gained from them (the cost-benefit ratio) that comes from how a manager handles each of those types of factors. *An effective supervisor gets a maximum cost-benefit ratio by managing material resources and by leading people.* The distinction between managing and leading separates the winners from the losers in the management game.

You manage your material resources. Material resources are inanimate—equipment, machinery, buildings, vehicles, supplies—everything physical needed for getting the job done, right down to the paper clips and rubber bands. You can do with them as you see fit. You can have your way with them in any manner that achieves the proper results. They don't think for themselves (not even computers); they don't have either business-related or private needs, wishes, or desires; they don't have problems, fears, or worries. Of course, you can abuse them. They're only as valuable as you or other people make them.

A supervisor is responsible for seeing to it that those resources are utilized properly, that they're used efficiently, that the company gets its dollar value—the greatest possible return on its investment—from each piece of equipment or every bit of the supplies. That's what I mean by managing your material resources.

On the other hand, to get the greatest possible return on the investment in people, you have to go about things very differently. Human resources are not inanimate, nor can you do with them as you see fit.

You know perfectly well that people think for themselves. You think for yourself, and you have no reason to doubt that other people do so, as well. And that ability, you'll see later, becomes an essential ingredient in your success in getting a significant return on the investment.

And yes, people have business-related and private needs, wishes, and desires. They have problems, fears, and worries. And they can be much more easily abused than can material resources. At the same time, when a machine is abused, it usually just breaks down and refuses to work. A human being, on the other hand, can abuse back by undermining, deliberately and maliciously, your ability to achieve your goal as supervisor. That's why a supervisor manages material things but leads people.

An ancient Chinese philosopher said that the art of effective leadership is getting people to do what you want them to do while letting them believe it was their idea in the first place. I'll take a simpler approach: *Leadership means the ability to mobilize the energies of other people toward the achievement of a goal or an objective that may or may not be in their own best interest.* It means getting them to want to do what you think is in their best interest. As a supervisor, a major portion of your job is to help people see the wisdom of doing their jobs properly and effectively and to help them maintain their motivation to do the very best they can. In short, *leadership in management means motivating other people to follow you.*

To sum up, then, leadership is at the heart of the manager's job. Informally defined, *management consists of getting effective results through the efforts of other people.* But you can't expect people to help you achieve your goals unless they want to. They won't want to unless you give them the incentive to work on your behalf. That's the finesse of leadership in management that most newly promoted supervisors lack.

Chapter 1

The Finesse of Leadership

Since what your people do can make or break you as a supervisor, your most important skill as a supervisor has little or nothing to do with your skill as a technician or craftsperson. Your most important management skill is *people handling*—how you treat the people who report to you, how you create an environment in which you, they, and the organization can meet the needs and requirements all three of you bring to the workplace. That's really how your performance will be judged.

Dolores has a head start on many other people. She was promoted largely on her well-known ability to get along with other people *and* get them to perform for her. The survival skills she needs in her personal life translate well into the workplace, but that's not enough. Instinct and/or personal experiences provide only a starting place for leadership in management.

The Attitudes of an Effective Supervisor

The traits of effective leadership include skills in planning, rational decision making, and communication. But more important, effective supervision depends upon attitudes: self-esteem and respect for others.

The attitudes and values the supervisor carries into the office affect the effectiveness of the people who work there. Belief in oneself and belief in the worth of the other people create a positive, productive environment in which everyone can feel creative and a part of the process.

Dolores's attitudes toward herself and the people in her unit make her adjustment easy. She believes in herself, and she believes in the others. They're good people. She says so herself.

Without self-esteem, you lock yourself into a box from the outset. In order to achieve whatever results you have targeted, you need first to believe that you've earned the right to pursue them; that you're a credible, capable human being; that you've worked for the position or the role you want in the group. That you believe you've earned the respect of other people allows you to occupy that position or that role.

Don't confuse self-esteem with egotism. The words *earned* and *worked for* play a crucial role in self-esteem. In this context, self-esteem means self-confidence—knowing that you're good at what you do, that you're a rational, reasonable, caring person. When you believe in yourself this way, it shows. Everyone else agrees with you without your having to ask them for their votes of confidence. In short, this form of self-esteem comes with the self-actualization I'll describe later.

Respect for others flows from self-esteem and vice versa. You can have little or no respect for yourself if you have little or no respect for other people. The respect you show for others becomes the basis for their showing you respect in return. And mutual re-spect—that's the basis for control.

The word *control* usually conjures up the specters of power, domination, ruling, governing, commanding, ordering, laying down the law, holding under a thumb—all negative concepts that produce negative feelings. Yet supervisors need to have control over their unit's actions, over the unit's work flow, and over the unit's output.

Control as mutual respect means having others agree with you, work with you, support you—willingly. They *want* to work for you, do their best for you because they respect you and because they know that you respect them as well. That's real control—when you can have other people follow you wherever you lead them.

That first Monday morning, when Dolores led her first unit meeting, after the greetings and the congratu-lations were finished, this is what she said to her "troops":

As far as I'm concerned, the major difference between last Friday and today is that I've got a new title—supervisor of auto claims. More than anything else, that title carries with it a whole lot of responsibility, but it won't cause a whole lot of

9

change in me. I'm still Dolores. I'm still an adjuster. I'm still one of you. Different in some respects, the same in others.

I'm different insofar as I have a lighter file load than before. I assign work. I authorize settlements when they exceed your authority limits. I review your files with you. I coach and I counsel. I hire people; and yes, I've got the authority to fire them, too.

But I'm the same inasmuch as I know you, I know how well you do your work. I trust you to do your work efficiently and effectively. I believe in your ability to exceed the goals set for us, to achieve more than our work standards require. I believe that you'll maintain the same level of morale we've always had. I believe that you'll help one another, you'll help me, and you'll help the new people as they come on board. In short, I believe that you'll make this the best unit to work in and the most productive unit in this company.

An effective supervisor begins with both self-esteem and a belief in the worth of his or her employees, in the ability of those employees to get the work done. Moreover, an effective supervisor believes that people, generally speaking, want to work and enjoy work that challenges them, that provides them with an opportunity to be creative, to use their minds and their talents. In fact, studies have shown that most people, even if they have independent wealth, will more than likely find some type of productive activity (work) to keep themselves busy and occupied.

Creating a Productive Environment

Your supervisory attitudes affect the outcome of the work people do. You create the culture of your unit, and it's that culture that produces the kind of climate in which you and your people will work. (See the accompanying sidebar.) If you treat people as people, not merely as material resources, they will perform for you.

The Culture of an Organization

Attitudes: The feelings people have toward things or other people—their readiness to respond favorably or unfavorably—and their expectations of how everyone should act.

Values: The things people like or don't like.

Aesthetics: The things they find beautiful.

Truths: The things in which they believe.

Mores: Their beliefs in right or wrong, good or bad.

Customs: The ways they do things.

People work best in a climate in which they are seen as co-workers, not merely as employees. They work best in a climate in which they are given a task to perform and then allowed to do it—even allowed to fail at doing it. They work best in a climate that recognizes their needs and feelings as well as their worth as human beings. They work best in a climate in which mutual respect and trust are the rule rather than the exception. Create a climate in which these factors are missing, or one in which you rule by force of personality, and you may hit some of your goals, but not all of them, and the price you may have to pay—through turnover and the like—could make achieving those goals a hollow accomplishment.

It's all well and good to say that you, the supervisor,

create the culture and climate of the unit. It's more important to explain to you how to be aware of how you do that.

First of all, keep in mind that your people see you as the authority in the group. Whatever goes on does so with either your actual or your tacit agreement or permission. Even those things that go on behind your back become your responsibility, because if you have the trust and loyalty of your group, nothing goes on behind your back.

You also have to keep in mind that a person comes to work for an organization on a voluntary basis, and people join groups through voluntary association because those groups meet their needs. Otherwise, the groups wouldn't be attractive to them. They therefore come to work motivated to do their very best because they expect that you and/or the organization will meet those needs.

It's a *psychological contract*—a set of beliefs or expectations. Should your employees feel that the contract is violated, they'll become demotivated and quit working, even if they don't physically leave their jobs.

At that morning meeting, whether or not she knew what she was doing, Dolores was producing the psychological contract that would govern her relationships with her people. And simultaneously, the psychological contract compounds Dolores's problems.

Remember that although everyone had jockied for the position, fortunately, everyone seemed to accept Dolores's promotion. As co-workers, they respected and trusted her. She was one of them. Their contract then, however, was among peers.

Now she's no longer one of them. What happens if she responds to her promotion as many people do—by wielding her authority with an iron fist? She violates two psychological contracts: the old one they had all built together over a number of years and the new one that she is trying to create now. The people lose their respect and trust for her, they become demotivated, they stop working productively, or they flatly walk off the job.

In their turn, Dolores and the organization have expectations, as well. From their side of the psychological contract, they require the loyalty and allegiance of the employees, their dedication to meeting the needs of the group. Though she will want them to be friendly, and she'll want to be friendly in return, she and the organization will expect their respect for her authority.

The respect for her authority *begins* with her status itself, the title to which she referred in her speech. What she does with it determines *how well* the people will respect it.

I'm touching on a problem that often befalls someone promoted from within the group to a position of authority over the group. Suddenly you've moved from being a co-worker and friend—another employee—to being a manager. The relationship you had with those people before is altered by the title, in spite of everything you try to do to prevent it. Status not only has its perks; it also has its price. You can expect to lose some of the warmth of your previous relationships if you fail to recognize that in spite of your title, you and the other people are still co-workers.

You still work toward a common goal, only now the common goal is yours—to achieve results through the proper utilization of your resources. These people are a part of your resources. By letting them do their jobs, by helping them do their jobs better, by treating them in accordance with the commonsense principle of the Golden Rule, you will not only retain the warmth that existed before, but moreover, you'll add to it.

Understanding, Integrating, and Balancing Needs

People, unlike machines, are animate, and that means they have needs that compel them to work—a need for survival, a need for security, a need to belong to a productive group, a need for personal recognition, a need for self-fulfillment, a need for a sense of personal power. Everyone has one or more of those needs that he or she tries to meet, but what compels a person to work varies from individual to individual.

Find out as quickly as possible your own drivers. Begin with your own needs, because the better you understand them, the better you'll be able to understand those of other people.

You don't need a Ph.D. in psychology to uncover what other people want or require as payoffs from their work. You need only to sharpen your powers of observation, to check out the needs that seem to underlie their behavior, and to assess both their assets and their liabilities. And though you don't have to be a psychologist, it doesn't hurt to look at what one psychologist, Abraham Maslow, said about human needs. While not the last word on motivation, it's a good first one.

Maslow identified what he called a hierarchy of needs, starting with the most basic: *physiological needs*—needs to be satisfied by food, clothing, shelter. They're the largest single group of needs and fairly well dominate work-related behavior. Though most people can, to a large extent, control them, these needs often drive their work life, and they do what they have to to meet them.

Impoverished people often see life only as a matter of basic survival. People totally preoccupied with meeting only these needs usually distrust anyone who could be seen as a threat to their livelihood. At the extreme are misers and other unsociable people whose basic needs are in fact being met but who believe that if they stopped hoarding and hiding their belongings, they would perish.

People driven by the second level of needs, *security (or safety) needs,* also defend themselves against anyone they see as a threat to their livelihood. These needs drive everyone to protect himself or herself against nature and other people. Everyone does what he or she can to keep the waters calm and smooth, to avoid disruption in the ordinary, daily affairs.

Carried to extremes in the workplace, this need shows up in people who don't want to take on new assignments, who don't want to be noticed by others, who want to be left alone to do their jobs—without what they call "hassles." They keep to themselves a great deal and sometimes become downright hostile if you try to involve them in activities that would possibly deny them their safety.

At the same time, though everyone at one time or another wants to be left alone, most people want to know that they're accepted and acceptable to the groups to which they belong, including their work groups. This third set of needs Maslow called *social needs:* caring for others and being cared for; being a friend, a colleague, a peer; depending on others, having other people depend on you. They all characterize social needs, and everyone does things to encourage people to meet his or her social needs.

Carried to extremes, we find people trying to meet these needs by being too friendly, too reasonable, too accommodating—absolutely terrified of interpersonal conflict or of negative feedback. Friendships are to be preserved at all costs, even if nothing is really threatening them.

Most industrial psychologists today agree with Maslow's contention that people work not merely for meeting survival needs but more for meeting social needs and the next two needs in the hierarchy: *ego needs* and *self-fulfillment needs*. Even if people had enough money to meet all their physiological and security needs, they'd still go looking for interesting, challenging, and exciting things to do. And studies show they'd go looking for them mostly in work-related activities, especially where they could maximize their contacts with other people.

So the fourth level of need Maslow identified, ego needs—the needs for independence, for influence, for dominance, for challenges, and recognition—compel many people to work. Anything that frustrates the satisfaction of that need is seen as a threat, and people do things to call attention to themselves. They demand the freedom to do what they do best with a minimum of supervision; they give advice and counsel (even if unsolicited); they attempt to lead the group whenever they can; they take on difficult tasks as long as those jobs don't seem to be overwhelming and unachievable; and when they meet those challenges, they want other people to notice their accomplishments.

In the extreme are egotists, the "oners" who demand rather than seek recognition. They're frequently argumentative, haughty, pompous, and grating. They lead by taking over the group, bullying it, threatening it, overwhelming it with the force of their personality or with their position of power in the group.

What's interesting about ego needs and the highest level of need—*self-fulfillment (or self-actualizing) needs*—is the similarities between them. They differ dramatically, however, in the quality of how people go about meeting those two sets of needs.

Self-actualizers also have a need for independence,

a need for influence, a need for dominance, a need for challenges, and a need for recognition. They differ from ego need–driven people in that they do what they do rationally, coolly, and with caring for other people. They also feel enough self-esteem not to have to demand the esteem of other people; self-recognition, self-satisfaction both suffice. Recognition from others takes second place.

When carried to extremes, this need for self-satisfaction turns into personal perfectionism, an intolerance for any flaw in one's own character or work.

These self-actualized people work well by themselves, but they also enjoy leading the group, which they do unobtrusively whether or not they have the formal title of manager. Their leadership is open and receptive to other people and involves listening to what they have to say, encouraging them to participate in the group's activities and decision-making process. They draw out the enthusiasm and creativity of the other members rather than demand obedience to their will. They are the center of communications, the ones to whom everyone else turns for accurate information. They quash rumors by getting at the facts and seeing to it that everyone else learns of them.

As leaders, self-actualized people are goal setters, helping the group plan logically and in order of priorities. They are the *organizers* who help others implement their plans. Their openness and honesty with other people evoke openness and honesty in return. Self-actualizers, because they draw out other people and allow them to participate and to contribute on their own initiative, are known in the group as *gatekeepers* and *enablers*.

Self-actualizers are gatekeepers, organizers, and enablers because they know better than most people that everyone has a need to experience *personal power,* which means that *everyone needs to feel competent and capable of meeting his or her own needs,* whatever those needs may be (physiological, security, social, ego, or self-fulfillment needs). People have to feel that they have some control over their lives. Self-fulfillment is the acme of exercising personal power, and self-actualizers recognize this need in everyone.

Ego need–driven people see only their own need for personal power and deny other people their right to theirs. Still, anytime you deny a person his or her right to exercise personal power (such as by embarrassing him or her in front of the group), you're just begging for trouble. One way or another, that person will retaliate, even if he or she appears to be a passive, security need–driven person or an unabashedly social need–driven person.

Dolores is a self-actualizer. She wants her position as her way of rewarding herself for the work she's done. But more important, she wants to succeed, and she will feel that she let herself down if she doesn't. After using Maslow's hierarchy of needs to find out what compels her to work, Dolores can use it to size up the people she now supervises.

Effective supervisors recognize that all people act on the basis of their personal needs. Those needs vary from person to person, but by and large, everyone acts on the basis of one or another, or some combination of, those six basic requirements that all human beings experience.

By watching how people act, by listening to what they say, you can frequently (but not always) judge fairly well what needs they are trying to meet. When you feel confident in your interpretation of their behavior, you'll have a better understanding of the whys and hows of their attitudes toward you, toward themselves, and toward their work, and this information will help you provide them the leadership they need.

A word of caution here: All comments about human needs are inferences—conclusions we draw about people by watching how they act and by listening to what they say. We see someone do something or hear him or her say something, and we conclude that he or she is trying to meet a certain need. We speak conclusively only about what we see, hear, touch, feel, and smell—and even then we're describing only our own impressions or interpretations of those sensory data.

This is why when you give *feedback*—that is, *when you tell someone how you're affected by what he or she does or says—you should (1) describe the behavior you've experienced, (2) tell the other person how you feel about it, and (3) tell him or her what you would like to see or hear in the future.* Giving and getting feedback constitute an important part of how you find out what people believe they want, as well as what they think and feel, and how you tell them about yourself.

To create a productive environment and draw from each employee the fullest of his or her potential, a supervisor has to find out what would move that person in the proper direction. As any good salesperson will tell you, people buy only when they see the benefit of the purchase to themselves.

How a Supervisor Motivates Employees

Since the whole person goes to work, the amount of productivity you get from any one person depends on how well you size up his or her needs and the payoffs he or she wants from and for the work performed.

A payoff is nothing more than the benefit or reward that a person hopes to gain by doing something, and payoffs come in two forms: tangible and intangible. Few supervisors have much control over the tangible benefits—such as wages, office arrangements, and so on—but they do have control over the intangible payoffs.

Recognition is an intangible payoff. Praise is an intangible payoff. Additional responsibility and authority are payoffs. Challenge is a payoff.

Not only do supervisors usually have little control over tangible rewards; they also have to guard against the bitter competition that can break out over them. Any group can tolerate some competition among its members. After all, because the rewards any group has to offer are limited, encouraging people to earn their share of the rewards is good for them and good for business. Competition, *in small doses,* helps everyone meet his or her own goals.

In most business organizations, tangible rewards are very limited. There are only so many dollars with which to pay salaries, only so many positions to offer for promotion, and so on. As long as people vie for those rewards without openly and deliberately trying to hurt one another, as they did when Dolores's position opened up, you, as a supervisor, can tolerate the competition, even create friendly competition within the group. Your objective is to help people meet their needs through payoffs they want or have to have while at the same time providing them with the incentives to meet the organization's goals and objectives.

It's when the competition becomes *one for one and none for all* that you have to clamp down on your employees. When they openly fight with one another for those rewards and do each other real harm, then you have to impose sanctions. You may even have to fire someone. That, too, is a supervisor's duty.

You not only have to integrate the needs of everyone

in the group with those of the organization; you also have to balance those needs against one another. Though the needs of the individual must always be considered, at times the needs of the organization must take priority over the needs of any one person. When an individual's needs clash with those of the group, and meeting the individual's needs would mean denying the group and the organization theirs, you have to take corrective action. Remember your mandate: to get your specific results in a given period of time.

A Strategy for Effective Leadership

Leadership. The common wisdom says it's something you're born with. I say, t'ain't necessarily so. All you need are the instincts of the run-of-the-mill, prehistoric cave dweller. It doesn't take anything special to see that one person alone with a spear won't drop a woolly mammoth to its knees. Even cave dwellers knew that economic survival depends on cooperation and teamwork. Cooperation and teamwork, in turn, depend on effective leadership.

Management requires skill in planning. You have to plan how the work will be done, who will do it, when, and where. For any action plan to be successful, a supervisor must have an overall strategy for how to handle the unit as a whole. Before Dolores came to work on that Monday, she designed a step-by-step plan for how she would handle any situation that arose. Dolores's seven steps fit into the four-part pattern of making any plan work: evaluate the data, set goals, design an action plan, and implement it.

First, in order to evaluate her situation, she had to find out her own goals. She needed to know what she was expected to accomplish with this group. She received good advice from John, when he told her to get results through the efforts of other people, but that wasn't enough. She needs to know *what* results he wants her to achieve—*specifics.*

Second, she begins to evaluate the data by assessing the dominant strategy of the organization as it relates to management style—how supervisors are supposed to treat employees. She has to know how the company wants her to act and how other people should act toward her.

Third, she has to assess the dominant way in which her people relate to each other. How do they see each other? What relationships and friendships exist in the group? How do these relationships affect their performance? How do those relationships fit with company policy? What would happen if she did something to disrupt those relationships?

Fourth, she'll also have to determine for sure what attitudes the people take toward her. Are they really satisfied that management did the right thing in promoting her? Is anyone hiding some angry feelings over the promotion? Are the subordinates willing to work with her and to follow her leadership? In short, the fourth part of the plan will require her to size up each of the people in the group and how each sees her as its newly appointed leader.

The fifth part of her strategy consists of assessing the strengths and weaknesses of each of her employees in order to decide how to assign tasks, to whom to delegate important responsibilities, and to whom to give special attention (coaching and counseling) in order to bring them up to speed.

The sixth part of her strategy consists of conscious decisions as to what to do to achieve her goals. This is the detailed action plan based on what results John expects from her. She has to plan the numbers of files they will need to close daily, weekly, monthly in order to reach their goals. She has to decide how to handle difficult claims. She has to plan her work assignments, her training programs, and so on. In short, she has to plan out the operations of her unit.

Finally, she has to consider how to win support from her employees for any changes or corrections she'll want to make in the way things are done, to place her imprint on the unit. She has to come up with a method that will raise their receptivity to her ideas and expectations rather than merely imposing her will and demanding obedience. She has to design an action plan that she can implement and that will work.

This is where knowing what her people want from and for their work makes the most difference. She can't sell them on her ideas unless she can figure out how those ideas will really benefit the other people as well as her and the company.

Understanding, integrating, and balancing needs requires a second skill: effective communication. That includes listening to other people as well as explaining yourself. In Chapter 2, I'll apply specific skill elements—inquiring, responsive listening, giving feedback, explaining, and resolving differences—to assessing employee needs and to explaining what you want from employees. In Chapter 3, I'll apply these skills to interviewing and hiring the right people.

Chapter 2

Communication Skills a Supervisor Must Have

You can't always rely on your interpretations of other people's behavior in order to assess what needs they're trying to meet. How, then, do you find out what would strike someone else's "on" buttons? Assessing their needs through observation is a good first step. Checking out the accuracy of your interpretation is the *necessary* next step, and it's one that requires effective communication skills.

Let's go back to Dolores's situation. One of the issues she has to confront is the possibility that someone is hiding some bad feelings about her promotion. After all, they all wanted the position, especially Mary. It's not too farfetched in our work world for someone to shelve feelings, pushing them aside but not really forgetting them, letting them explode at a later, very inopportune, date. If Mary has a real problem, Dolores can correct the situation to some extent. If it isn't a real problem, they can at least clear the air and get on with business. The only way for Dolores to find out if something is really eating Mary is to check it out.

Checking things out is a good example for use in this chapter because it includes many different features of effective communication: *structuring, probing, listening, explaining, resolving differences,* and *achieving closure.*

Dolores structures all of her discussions with employees in the same manner—whether for coaching and counseling, for assigning work, for resolving a problem, or for appraising performance. First, she sets an informal tone to the meeting through a *friendly opening,* which includes making light conversation, making a statement of the purpose of the meeting, and getting a commitment from the other person to work toward a common outcome from the meeting.

She then *elicits* the opinions, beliefs, or feelings of the other person about the issue they're considering before she takes the third step, which is to *explain* her point of view. Fourth, they resolve differences of opinion before going on to the fifth step, which is to *achieve closure*—agreeing on an action plan for doing something or for taking corrective action with respect to a problem, or just making sure everyone understands each other, and so on.

The structure of the discussion is only as effective as the tools you use for getting the conversation to flow toward a goal you set for yourself and the other person. Keep in mind, also, that the effectiveness of the conversation depends upon the level of trust that you've been able to generate with your employees. Without that trust, you'll never be able to achieve the candor you need for open and honest discussions.

You check things out by asking *open-ended questions,* questions that begin with *who, what, why, where, when,* and *how.* Those questions require the other person to elaborate at least somewhat on his or her answer. Questions that produce a dead-end answer begin with *are you, will you, do you, can you, would you, should you,* and so on. They're *closed-end questions,* which end a discussion or verify a point of fact.

Closed-ended questions require a yes or no answer. Open-ended questions can't be answered by yes or no. Someone asks, "How's the project going?" It would seem a bit strange to answer, "Yep." Or, "What's the weather like out there?" "Nope."

Probing questions spoken pleasantly and with a genuine interest in getting at the truth, at reality, at feelings, or in finding solutions to problems usually get the desired results. Not in every case, to be sure, but in most cases.

Closely related to open-ended and closed-ended questions are open-ended and closed-ended *comments.* "I'd like to hear more about that." "Tell me what you think about what I've said." Those are open-ended comments. They encourage the other person to talk freely about the subject at hand. A yes or no answer wouldn't be appropriate.

"You seem to have made up your mind." "You're O.K. with that." Those are closed-ended comments designed to verify a fact or to get agreement on something. Yes or no answers are appropriate in response to these remarks.

Another way to get information from someone is to sit in *pregnant silence.* Make a comment, ask a question, and shut up. Wait for an answer. Nature abhors a vacuum, our science teachers taught us. Well, so do people. And silence is a kind of vacuum. You'll get a reply if only you'll wait. This is particularly effective with people who tend to protect their security needs excessively.

Pregnant silence, *a deliberate stop in the flow of the conversation,* is less threatening than, "I'm talking to you, and I'd appreciate a response." Verbally pushing a protective person to talk will usually get the opposite reaction. Have you any teenage children? Then you probably know exactly what I mean.

An important way of advancing a discussion is to give feedback. *Informational feedback* refers to repeating, in your own words, what you think the other person said or describing what the other person did. *Behavioral feedback* describes what a person has said or done and how it has affected you. Whereas you use informational feedback to let the other person know you understand or want to be corrected in what you think you understand, behavioral feedback is usually used to get someone to repeat an action you liked or to stop doing something you didn't like.

A third form of feedback is *mirroring,* reflecting back to the other person the emotion or feelings you detect in what the person has said or done. Mirroring is used to get the other person to ventilate the feelings (whatever they may be)—to get the emotions out of the way. That way he or she can talk openly and honestly to satisfy whatever caused the anger, if anger is the emotion, or get on with business, if excitement or pleasure is the emotion.

A brief dialog between Dolores and Mary will help illustrate (1) how Dolores structures the discussion and (2) how she uses the basic elements of effective communication.

Opening

Dolores: Thanks for giving me a few minutes of your time. It gets so, sometimes, that I don't seem to be able to talk with anyone anymore. At least we get to go to lunch together this week, since you're on the early rotation.

Mary: It does make a difference. I'm glad you changed the system. It makes it a little easier on all of us to know that we don't always have to take the same shift each week.

Dolores: Everyone seems to like it. Eventually, I'll be in a position to put myself in the rotation and get to go to lunch with everyone once in a while. But, Mary, I asked for this meeting because I'd like to check out something with you. We've always been able to talk openly and honestly with each other, and I've appreciated that and come to respect our relationship because of it. [*Pregnant silence*]

Mary: I've always felt the same way. Check out what?

Dolores: I know you really wanted the promotion as much as I did, and before things go too far, I'd like an up-front discussion of it. How do you feel about doing this? [*Open-ended question*]

Mary: I think it's a good idea. I figured you'd be wondering about it. And I'd like to set the record straight, too.

Eliciting the Other's Views

Dolores: I'm glad you feel that way. What are you feeling about my promotion? [*Open-ended question*]

Mary: Right now, pleased for you—pleased for us. I think it was the right choice. You're good at whatever you do.

Dolores: Right now, you're feeling O.K. about the change. [*Mirroring*] How did you feel before? [*Open-ended question*]

Mary: As you said, we've always been open and honest with each other. Well, I was miffed. I felt like quitting. I really wanted and needed the promotion. I think I can do the job, and we need the extra income.

Dolores: So, at first, you felt upset [*Mirroring*] be-

	cause you felt passed over and need more money. [*Informational feedback*] Is that right? [*Closed-ended question*]
Mary:	That's right. But I'm over it now.
Dolores:	You're sure. [*Closed-ended comment*] I'd like to know more about your feelings. [*Open-ended comment*]
Mary:	I appreciate your concern, Dolores, but really, there's nothing more to say.
Dolores:	I respect your candor, and I won't push that issue. Thanks for your support, too. But I'd like to talk about something you're not pursuing. [*I-statement*] Is that O.K.? [*Closed-ended question*]

Explaining Your Viewpoint

Mary:	What is it? Did I do something wrong?
Dolores:	No. Not at all. It's the matter of needing extra income. I'm not going to pry into your private life, but I am concerned that if things are really bad, you might get angry again that you didn't get the position, or you might have to take an evening job that could interfere with your work here, or that anxiety will interfere with the way you do your job. [*I-statement*] What do you think of my concerns? [*Open-ended question*]
Mary:	I don't think you have anything to worry about.

Resolving a Disagreement

Dolores:	Maybe we should talk about it a little more. I have the feeling that you're a bit upset about what I've said. [*Mirroring*]
Mary:	Well, a little. Things at home are a bit

Dolores: tough, and I really don't want to go into them in detail. I'd like to just drop the whole matter.

Dolores: Mary, I don't want to go into the details. I understand you don't want to share personal things here, and I respect your right to privacy. [*Informational feedback*] I'm a little distressed that you thought I was being nosy, because I'm interested only in how we might be able to help you move upward along a technical career path or into a supervisory position in another unit. [*Behavioral feedback*]

Mary: I guess I did get a bit snappish. I really do appreciate your concern. If there's a way to get ahead faster than what I'm doing now, I sure do want to know about it.

Dolores: Then you want to talk about it now while the subject's hot? [*Closed-ended question*]

Mary: If you can spare the time.

Achieving Closure

Dolores: I can. If you're ready to talk about it, let's start by finding out what you're looking for in your work. [*Open-ended comment*]

That's enough of that compressed, artificial conversation, but you can see how to use the different elements of effective communication to get at information that opens up a problem about which Dolores might not have known anything and that could have risen up to blindside her at some time or another.

Structuring your meetings, using appropriate questions, using pregnant silence, and giving informational or behavioral feedback and/or using mirroring are important communication skills. To these, I'll add a few other dimensions to the idea of effective communication.

A Six-Part Method for Communicating Effectively

A set of methods helps structure the basic tools of effective communication into a workable pattern. The first part is self-expression; the second, responsive listening; the third, acknowledging; the fourth, understanding; the fifth, completeness; the sixth, closure.

Self-expression—the word should be relatively self-explanatory. It refers to the way in which you convey what you believe or feel. When discussing problems or issues that crop up in a workplace, most people pay little attention to how they phrase their messages. The upshot is that they sometimes create problems where before they had none because they said something, or were understood to have said something, they hadn't intended.

You probably noticed, in the dialog earlier, a phrase in brackets: "I-statement." You can avoid many verbal conflicts merely by learning to use two different ways of expressing yourself: *I-statements* and *You-statements.*

With I-statements, you take ownership of your feelings or beliefs by referring to yourself in the statement. For example, "I believe management treated me shabbily, and I'm angry over it." "I'm pleased that you've agreed to work with me on this project because I think we'll both benefit from the collaboration." "It seems to me that something is wrong with the way people relate to one another here."

Contrast those statements with what are called You-statements: "You treated me shabbily." "You'll get a lot out of working on this project." "You people relate to one another badly."

Most of the time, You-statements accuse people of doing, thinking, or feeling things. They give the impression that you assume that what you believe is necessarily true. They tend to produce bad feelings. The most effective use of You-statements is when they compliment the other person (and then you run the risk of seeming to be patronizing). "You did a great job on those files, Bob." "By coming in early, you got a lot of those files closed ahead of schedule."

In addition to expressing themselves, great communicators listen attentively to everything people say to them. They use the skill called *responsive listening*. It refers to giving your complete attention by clearing both the area around you and your mind at the same time. It refers to making sure you've understood what the other person said by asking questions for clarification or by paraphrasing. Paraphrasing also lets the other person know that you're listening and that you're trying to understand (even if, in fact, you don't understand).

Listening without understanding wastes everyone's time. Asking questions for clarification not only shows that you're trying to understand but, ultimately, results in your gaining a complete understanding.

I-statements play a very important role in responsive listening: "If I understood you. I think you said . . ." The message says clearly that you have assumed the responsibility of trying to understand the other person.

Giving and asking for feedback are powerful tools for demonstrating that you understand or, conversely, for finding out if the other person understands you.

Another way to show the other person that you're listening is to *acknowledge* what the other person seems to you to be feeling, either by mirroring or by letting the other person ventilate. You'll recall that earlier Dolores did both when talking with Mary about her feelings.

Feedback and acknowledgment not only demonstrate or confirm understanding but ensure *completeness* as well. Once you're convinced that you and the other person do understand each other, it's important to check out whether everything that you intended to include or should have included in the conversation has been communicated. For example, you could ask, "What else should we talk about before we end this meeting?" Or, "I think we've covered the waterfront. How do you see it?"

If the parties to the discussion agree on all aspects of it, you're reaching *closure*. This is reflected by statements such as, "I think I see what you mean, and I'll try to do what we agreed on." Or, "To be sure I communicated what I meant, I need some feedback, please." (Contrast the second statement with, "Do you understand?")

The entire method assumes two important ingredients: (1) that you have the right to be heard and understood and (2) that you respect the same right for other people. Self-esteem and respect for others—the basic attitudes of supervision and leadership.

Chapter 3

Hiring the Right People

Skilled communicators make the best interviewers because they know how to structure a discussion to get the information they need, how to probe for the answers they have to have, how to listen responsively to the answers, how to explain the nature and responsibilities of the job, and how to achieve closure. All these elements go into a good hiring interview.

As mentioned, Dolores has to hire two people—one to replace her and an additional person. The company recruits for openings two ways: by open posting for people within the company to get a crack at the slots and by advertising in the newspapers. Personnel screens the applicants before sending the paperwork on to Dolores for her interviews. So in advance of the interviews, Dolores has (1) a completed application, (2) a résumé, and (3) in the case of an internal transfer, the applicant's personnel folder. To these standard documents, Dolores adds one of her own. It's called an *interview guide.*

The interview guide provides additional structure to the discussion. Dolores uses her openers to set the applicant at ease. Then she begins the most important part of the process. She gets the applicant to present himself or herself first before explaining the position.

Many interviewers make the mistake of describing the position first, which tells the applicant what answers the interviewer wants to hear rather than giving an accurate picture of the applicant's true ability to do the job.

Only after Dolores gets a clear image of the applicant's qualifications and decides that this person is worth pursuing does she go into detail about the position and the career path to which it pertains. She explains only as much as she thinks is warranted in the situation. If she really isn't giving the applicant that much consideration, she tells the person only enough to give him or her a polite brush-off. When appropriate, she tells the applicant that she isn't considering him or her at all.

If any misunderstandings or differences of opinion arise between her and the applicant, especially if she is giving this candidate real consideration, she'll clear up those problems before bringing the interview to a close, ending by (1) explaining the next steps in the process and (2) checking to see whether the applicant is really interested in the position. No sense in proceeding if he or she isn't.

By following the basic structure of any of her business discussions and by using the interview guide, she gets all the information she needs for matching the applicant's qualifications against the demands and requirements of the job.

In the sidebar on pages 36–37, you'll find an abbreviated sample interview guide based on Dolores's need to replace herself with an experienced all-lines claims adjuster. In it, you see that she has two lists: one is labeled "Requirements" and the other is labeled "Qualifications." Each list is divided into subheadings: "Education and Training," "Knowledge," "Experience," "Skills Needed," "Personal Characteristics/Traits," "Ability to Deal with People." (You could also set up these lists as two columns, side by side, that is, as a T-chart.) In each subsection of the guide, Dolores lists either questions to ask or requirements of the job to which the questions relate. Now read that interview guide before continuing.

With some idea of what the guide looks like (whether or not you understand any of the technical terms), you can see that all the questions are job-related, and while some personal questions are asked, they, too, are job-related. Dolores has two reasons for structuring her interview that way: Her only real interest in the applicant at this point is whether or not he or she can do the job and fit into their environment, and Equal Employment Opportunity legislation demands that interviews be keyed to the job and job standards in order to prevent unfair hiring or promotion practices.

Interview Guide

Requirements

Knowledge

How to evaluate a liability claim.
How to evaluate an injury claim.
How to settle a claim properly.
How to litigate a claim.

Skills Needed

Ability to evaluate statements.
Ability to negotiate a settlement.
Ability to analyze data and draw sound conclusions.
Ability to use proper resources to research a problem.

Ability to Deal with People

In control of oneself during stressful situations.
Capable of managing the emotions of other people in
    stressful situations.
Capable of working in a team environment.
Able to take direction and correction.

Qualifications

Experience

Describe the work you've done for Company X.
What is the organizational structure in which you work?
How do you evaluate a claim?
If your authority limit is $3,500 and the claim exceeds
    your limit, what do you do?
What basic steps do you take to evaluate the following
    claim: medical special of $3,000 and wage loss of
    $5,000?

Education and Training

What in your college education prepared you for this
   type of work?
What additional training for this type of work have you
   had and from where?

Personal Characteristics/Traits

What did you like and dislike about your supervisors
   and/or co-workers?

In any interview, in order of importance, the information you need includes work experience, education and
training, and personal history. Especially in her case,
Dolores asks about work experience first because
she's looking for an experienced adjuster. When interviewing a person without experience, you might ask
about education and training first, but the person's
work history still gives you a better idea of whether or
not he or she can do the job you want done. *You need
to get at the essentials first, ask the knockout questions early in order to save yourself a lot of wasted
time.*

Notice that almost all her questions are open-ended.
Dolores doesn't ask, "Can you work on your own?"
She asks instead, "What is the organizational structure
in which you work?" Rather than ask, "Have you
handled bodily injury claims?" she asks, "Describe the
work you've done for Company X."

Dolores uses a relatively complicated question in the
guide as a *knockout question.* She has several of
them, but with this one, she really tests whether the
applicant's personal claims are true—"What basic
steps do you take to evaluate the following claim:
medical special of $3,000 and wage loss of $5,000?"

The manner of the question omits much data needed for a straightforward answer. No answer is better than any answer. Another pair of dialogs will show you how important it is for you to use this type of question.

Dolores: Paul, since you said your authority limits are $3,500, what do you do at Company X when a settlement exceeds that?

Paul: I have to get clearance from the manager.

Dolores: What, then, are the basic steps for evaluating a situation in which you have a medical special for $3,000 and wage loss of $5,000?

Paul: I'd probably settle for $25,000 and get clearance.

Dolores: Well, thank you for applying, Paul. We'll notify you in at least one week whether or not you get the position.

Even if you don't understand the technical language, after you read the next discussion, you'll see why Dolores rejects Paul and considers Alice, whose authority to settle a claim is also limited to $3,500.

Dolores: What, then, are the basic steps for evaluating a situation in which you have a medical special for $3,000 and wage loss of $5,000?

Alice: I don't think I can answer the question as it's posed. I need more information. For example, what were the injuries? To what extent did they disable the claimant? For how long? Data like that. Only then could I decide on a settlement.

Dolores: You'd need more information, then.

Alice: Of course. It's my job to evaluate the claim carefully, on the basis of all the data I can get, before deciding on a fair settlement.

Alice gave the right answer to that question. Paul jumped too quickly to quoting a settlement amount. That demonstrated to Dolores either a lack of experience or a lack of judgment. In either case, he wasn't the right person for this job.

I'm sure you get the picture by now. Your job as a supervisor requires you to hire the right people for the jobs available. You need to find out if the person under consideration is the right person. To do that, you have to ask the questions and let the candidate do most of the talking—80 percent of it, in fact. A good interview with a likely candidate should take at least an hour and a half, after which he or she should be the one all talked out.

The 20 percent of the interview that is your responsibility comes mostly from the interview guide—the "Requirements" column. Since the material comes from the job description, it is complete and accurate, and it should give the candidate enough information on which to base his or her decision to accept or reject the opportunity.

After the job description, you add a bit of history about the company, an outline of company benefits, policies and practices, and so on. The objective is to make the company attractive to a viable candidate—to sell him or her on the position—in order to prevent making an offer and being turned down. This part of the interview also begins the process of creating the psychological contract because it identifies many of the requirements the candidate will come to expect and on which he or she will base the decision to come to work for you.

To find out if the person is interested in the position, you ask questions such as, "What are you looking for in a position?" "What do you want to do with your career?" Then, before wrapping up the interview, encourage the candidate to ask you specific questions that you can answer. The questions asked and the reactions to the answers can tell you just how interested he or she really is, especially if you end your answers with questions like, "How does that sound to you?"

Directness doesn't hurt, either. Bring it all to a close by asking, "If we decide to extend the offer, do you think you will accept?" If the answer is yes, you can then ask, "If we decide to extend the offer, when could you start?" Now, if you think you want to hire this candidate, you know whether or not you should extend the offer.

Effective communication skills. Without them, a supervisor really can't do his or her job.

Chapter 4

Decision Making and Problem Solving

Picking the right candidate for the job involves both problem-solving skills and decision-making skills. The problem is filling the position with the right person. The decision is selecting the right person for the job.

Actually, little separates solving a problem from making a decision. Solving a problem means *choosing the right alternative action to resolve some difficulty*—for example, how to assign the proper workload to people with different skills and abilities—whereas making a decision means *choosing between alternatives, period.*

The steps for making the proper choices are essentially the same for both problem solving and decision making:

1. Identify the basis for making a decision.
2. Collect all the relevant data needed for making it.
3. Analyze the data.
4. Identify the alternative courses of action.
5. Identify the contingencies related to each alternative.
6. Weigh the alternatives.
7. Select one course of action for trial.

The only significant difference comes at the first step: In solving a problem, the basis for making the decision is always to overcome a specific perceived difficulty. Therefore, I'll illustrate the whole process of decision making by talking about solving a specific problem.

Sometimes, the process begins with merely a sense that something's not right. You can't put your finger on it, but you know something's wrong. In a business situation, problem solving doesn't often start that way, but it can.

Usually, a business problem begins with some pretty solid evidence that something's out of whack: goals not being met, high rate of absenteeism, high rate of turnover, expenses exceeding income, and so on. Those are all *symptoms* of problems. Too often, managers look at the symptoms and leap to half-baked solutions before finding out the causes.

Dolores has a problem, a relatively simple one, that helps illustrate the decision-making process. Allen—her youngest, least experienced adjuster—is having trouble closing his daily quota of files, and recently, he has started coming in late and taking too long at lunch.

He's falling further and further behind, and his performance is hurting the overall performance of the group.

The easiest answer would be—"Allen, get to work on
time, take your hour for lunch, close your files on
schedule, or you're fired." That might not be the best
answer, however.

A harsh response like that might just make matters
worse. Instead, Dolores uses her communication skills
(1) to get Allen's commitment to solve the problem, (2)
to get Allen to identify the causes of the problem, (3) to
get Allen to help find the solution, and (4) to get Allen to
make the commitment to take corrective action. A short
dialog will illustrate both how Dolores does all that and
the steps to use for solving any problem or for making a
decision.

As you're reading this, keep something else in mind
also. Coaching and counseling are really special cases
of problem solving and decision making. The best
coaches *help you solve your own performance problems* rather than solve them for you. What you're about
to read is as much a coaching session as it is a
problem-solving activity.

Getting Commitment from an Employee
to Solve a Problem

Dolores: [*After a brief, pleasant conversation to set
Allen at ease and reassure him that he's
not "in trouble"*] Allen, I've asked you to
talk with me because I need your help to
solve a problem. It seems to me you're
having trouble closing your files and with
your punctuality. Those are problems for
me because it's my responsibility to see to
it that the work gets out smoothly and with
a minimum of stress in the unit. Do you

	think you can help me identify the causes
	of these problems and correct them?
Allen:	I really don't know. I do know what it is
	you're talking about, but I have some things
	to work out for myself to get things right
	again.
Dolores:	In other words, you do want to help me, but
	you're not sure that you can.
Allen:	I guess so.
Dolores:	You do see the benefit to you if we can
	solve this problem.
Allen:	I won't get canned.
Dolores:	Well, I wouldn't go that far in this particular
	matter, but you do realize that your per-
	formance review and your merit increase
	will be affected by this situation. So I be-
	lieve it's really in your best interest to get at
	a solution.
Allen:	Sure. I'll do what I can to get my work done
	on time.

Up to this point, Dolores has demonstrated that the problem belongs to both of them and that she's willing to work with Allen if he's willing to work with her. She's also shown him what's in it for him if he corrects the problem. Therefore, she has gotten his commitment for making the effort.

Now she turns to uncovering the real problem underlying the symptoms. The next piece of dialog will be truncated to spare you the details of what a claims adjuster has to do to close a file. What's important is how Dolores gets Allen to start talking by reassuring him again that she's on his side and by asking him to review his own assessment of the situation. Finally, she summarizes what she thinks he said before offering her own opinion.

Notice also that everything they talk about penetrates to issues behind the symptoms. They're not talking about late files or tardiness. They're talking about *why* the files aren't closed on time and *why* he's coming in late.

Identifying the Problems

Dolores: You really don't have to work it out by yourself as you said. That's why I'm here—to help you. Why don't we talk it out? What do you think is behind all this?

Allen: I've tried to sort it out many times, but I don't seem to be able to complete a file as quickly as the others. Maybe I'm spending too much time talking with the claimants. Sometimes . . .

Dolores: So, if I understand what you're saying, you think you spend too much time talking with the claimants; sometimes, especially if they're angry, you let them ventilate a lot, but then you don't know how to respond—you feel intimidated. If I remember correctly, you also said . . . Have I got all of that right, Allen?

Allen: I guess so, and because I'm doing so poorly, I'm having trouble psyching myself up to get here on time, and when I go to lunch, I really don't want to come back.

Dolores: So you think your poor performance discourages you.

Allen: I guess that's it.

Dolores: Would it be safe to say that if you improved your performance, you'd eliminate the tardiness problems?

Allen: Probably.

Dolores: I'm inclined to agree with everything you said, but I think we may have to deal with one or two other issues before we move

Allen: on. I think from what I see in your files that you're still not too clear on some of the regulations in some of the states in which we're operating or on some of our own policies governing insurable risks. Either you are letting mistakes lie and correcting them after I review the file, or you're spending too much time researching them. What do you think of my analysis?

Allen: Seems pretty right on.

Now Dolores and Allen have discussed the symptoms and uncovered the problems. The data they've come up with include Allen's own evaluation of how he deals with difficult claim situations and Dolores's evaluation of the technical details involved in his files. Together they've developed a relatively complete list of factors on which they can work to correct the problem. Their next step is to identify the possible solutions to the problem—select the proper alternative steps for arriving at something that works.

As you read this next piece of dialog, take notice of how Dolores gets Allen to develop the possible solutions before she offers a suggestion of her own. Only by involving an employee in the problem-solving process can you get his or her commitment to implement and follow through on the plan. After all, it's his or her solution, isn't it?

Selecting Alternatives

Dolores: Well, what do you think we can do about all this?

Allen: I suppose as far as the regs and policies go, I'd better do a little more homework. That's the easy part, but I really don't know what to do about the way I feel when a claimant jumps all over me.

Dolores:	Is it possible that they might go together?
Allen:	I'm not sure of what you mean.
Dolores:	Think about it a minute.
Allen:	Oh, wait. You're saying that if I were more sure of the regs and policies, I wouldn't be as easily intimidated.
Dolores:	That's possible. What do you think we can do about it?
Allen:	As I said, I'd better do more homework.
Dolores:	That's one alternative solution, but I wonder if that's enough.
Allen:	What else?
Dolores:	Let's look at it and weigh it against the situation. Regs and policies are facts. When you know your facts, you at least can give the right answers, but when an angry claimant is shouting at you, you get extremely stressed. You said so yourself. When you're stressed like that, what happens to your ability to remain calm and deal with nothing but the facts?
Allen:	It goes down the tubes. You're right, Dolores. I need something more than just a book of facts.
Dolores:	So?
Allen:	Could you help me? You're so darned cool under fire. Surely there are some tricks you can teach me.
Dolores:	Most of it seems to come just from experience, but there are some things I do consciously, and I can share some of those. First. . . .

During this third step, they work possible solutions to Allen's stress problems. Unlike in this example, you sometimes have to reject alternatives that either you or your employee proposes. Not all solutions fit the problem. In this case, the employee's solution fit but was insufficient in itself. Dolores helped him come up with an additional step. All that's left is for them to work out an action plan that will bring Allen's performance up to standards—an action plan that includes deadlines for getting on track and consequences if he doesn't achieve the proper results. With that, they achieve closure.

Naturally, not all problems are that easy to solve, and not all problems permit you to involve your employees. Sometimes you have to make decisions by yourself. The sidebar will show you some criteria for when to involve others. Regardless of whether or not you involve other people, you follow the same steps that you've just seen in making a decision. Distinguish between symptoms and causes, weigh the alternatives, decide on which action to take.

- -

When to Involve Others in Decisions You Have to Make

1. If time permits discussion and analysis. That is, if you don't have to have the decision immediately.
2. If the decision affects the personal or business lives of the employee(s). At least their input and feedback will help you make a mutually acceptable decision.
3. If the problem you have stems from the behavior of another person, and only that person's corrective action will solve your problem.
4. If you accept final responsibility for a decision that has been given to you and not to the others, but collective discussion would yield a better solution than by mulling it over on your own.
5. If responsibility for the decision can be shared by

the group with no one person's being held liable if
a decision that seems right turns out not to work
after all.
6. If data available to others are not available to you,
or if their expertise will help you solve the problem.
7. If implementation requires group commitment
and effort.

Chapter 5

Progress Review and Performance Appraisal

I said at the outset of the problem-solving dialog in the
previous chapter that, in a real sense, problem solving
with an employee is a form of coaching or counseling.
It is also, in a real sense, a progress review. Seen
another way, unless your employees perform perfectly
at all times, all progress reviews include problem solving—and decision making, and coaching or counseling, and action planning.
   The process is continuous and constant. It's your job
as a supervisor to get results through the efforts of
other people, right? Therefore, you have to know what
results you expect them to achieve, how they're supposed to achieve them, and by when. Your main activity relative to all that is to monitor your people's progress toward their goals, catch problems before they

become crises, and take corrective action when needed—or reward people for their accomplishments. An "atta boy" or "atta girl" at the right moment goes a long way toward urging people to do even better.

Performance appraisal is a process or group of activities over time rather than a periodic event. That process consists of setting goals or objectives or work standards, monitoring work during a given period of time, and reviewing progress both informally and formally. That's what you saw Dolores doing with Allen.

They discussed (1) Allen's not closing enough files and (2) his not coming in to work or back from lunch on time. That implies (1) that Dolores has given Allen a specific number of files to close and (2) that the company has policies with respect to tardiness. In short, Allen has been given objectives to achieve and work standards to uphold. Those are the basis for evaluating whether or not an employee has performed up to minimum standards or has exceeded them.

Whether your company uses a system in which you and your employees can set minimum goals or it sets them down for you, you need goals and objectives and work standards as the bases for conducting progress reviews and performance appraisals. They're the only objective measures you have. Any other assessments can be no more than subjective. Both you and your employees have to know exactly what's expected of them before they can meet those expectations. Therefore, at the beginning of any review period, you and your employees must sit down together to discuss their goals, objectives, and other standards.

The goals and standards must include targets to be hit, deadlines by when they will be hit, methods that will be used to hit them, and what to do if something should happen to get in the way of hitting them (that is, how to handle contingencies). What the employee can expect from you by way of help in hitting the targets is another important element, and when he or she can expect to have a formal review with respect to specific targets should be included, as well.

You distinguish formal from informal progress reviews easily enough. First, you plan a formal progress review for a specific date. Informal reviews are spontaneous. Second, you identify in advance specific targets and activities to be covered in a formal progress review. You deal with whatever problem arises or you reward for any achievement that occurs at the moment during an informal review. Third, you and your employee both know that a formal progress review carries with it the weight of an appraisal. Comments you and/or your employee make during an informal review may or may not resurface during the formal, final appraisal.

The dialog between Dolores and Allen illustrates a formal progress review. Here's an example of an informal review. This comes 48 hours after their previous conversation. They're sitting in the break room having a cup of coffee together.

Dolores: I see you haven't been late once since we spoke, and you seem more relaxed. How are you feeling about things now?

Allen: Much better. Thanks for your help.

Dolores: Thank you. You're helping me as much as I'm helping you. Keep up the good work.

Did that conversation take 30 seconds? Maybe less, but it was a progress review nonetheless. They discussed how Allen was doing with respect to correcting the tardiness problem. Dolores may not have seen that conversation as a comment on Allen's work, but let me assure you, Allen did. A supervisor's perceptions of a situation and those of his or her employees may not always coincide.

Reviews such as those, and formal reviews, go on

throughout the rating period. A clear and accurate record of those reviews makes a formal performance appraisal easy to write and easier to discuss. A *critical-incident file* kept on *each employee* gives you the clear and accurate record you need.

The word *critical* in "critical-incident file" means *important*. The file contains memos; informal comments noted for the record; responses by the employee; commendations or other comments about the employee from other people, such as your boss or customers; and so on. If you have a work-measurement system in your unit, the file contains the ongoing record of what the employee has achieved in this regard. When it comes time to write the formal appraisal, these items become the data that you plug into the appraisal itself.

Between the data in the file and the informal and formal progress reviews, the final performance appraisal contains absolutely no surprises. Rather, the formal appraisal consists of a *recap* of everything you've already discussed with the employee, plus a discussion of the goals, objectives, and standards to be achieved during the next rating period and, if possible, steps to take to advance the employee along a career path.

You've probably guessed by now that the same structure for holding any work-related conversation applies to both the progress review and the performance appraisal. Cover the openers, get commitment from your employee to deal with the territory under consideration, hear out your employee's viewpoint, explain yours, resolve disagreements, and work out an action plan to continue to improve performance. The same communication skills that help you become successful at problem solving, decision making, and hiring the right people help you conduct a progress review or performance appraisal.

Conclusion

Becoming a supervisor, especially being promoted into that role from within the ranks of the group you're to supervise, presents many challenges and can be frightening. Just remember what Dolores's boss told her: a supervisor's only mandate is to achieve results through the efforts of other people.

You have choices as to how you'll achieve those results: you can try to bully your employees, let your employees do as they please as long as they don't make waves, or lead your employees. Maintaining your self-esteem and having respect for your people produce leadership, and leading your employees usually gets the best results.

But leadership requires effective communication. Effective communication, in turn, requires understanding why your people have come to work (what they see as their payoffs). It requires responsiveness to their needs. It requires responsive listening to understand their needs and their perceptions of the world in which you all work. It requires skill in explaining your viewpoint clearly, accurately, and empathetically. It requires a willingness to resolve differences as well as an ability to do so. It requires an ability to achieve closure from which both you and the other person come away satisfied that both your needs have been met.

Leadership in management also means hiring the right people for the jobs to be done. Too often managers hire someone because they like that person, whether or not he or she is appropriately skilled. They hire on the basis of chemistry, or they hire in their own image.

You need to take care to avoid such subjective bases for making hiring decisions. A carefully planned interview, anchored by a detailed interview guide, will help you make the right hiring decisions.

Making the right decisions—that's another mark of leadership in management. Sometimes you need to involve others in helping you make those decisions, sometimes not, but in either case, you can't make the right decisions (or solve problems) unless you follow all the steps.

Identify the causes (not just the symptoms) of the problem. Analyze all the relevant data. Identify a number of possible solutions or alternatives for action (not just one). Weigh each one against the conditions and contingencies of the situation. Select the one alternative that seems to fit the situation best. Test it for a given period of time, and if it doesn't work, move on to another of those possible solutions or alternatives. And remember, that's what coaching and counseling are all about, as well.

Finally, as a leader in management, you have to monitor, review, and appraise the work of the people you lead. You need to know what you expect from them, and they need you to communicate those expectations to them, clearly, concisely, and accurately. That's part of the psychological contract you create with them.

Continuous and regular progress reviews keep your employees on track or correct their course should they deviate from the plan. Continuous and regular progress reviews build a bond between you and your employees. You change your role from that of peer and friend to friendly manager and leader. Your interest is theirs and vice versa.

All in all, effective leadership in management comes down to this. Respect your employees, create a productive environment in which you, they, and the company can achieve your goals, and your employees will respect you. Out of that mutual respect, all of you, working together, will achieve the results you are all expected to achieve. And that's your mandate, isn't it?

Suggested Readings

Belker, Loren B., *The First-Time Manager: A Practical Guide to the Management of People.* New York: AMACOM, 1986 (2nd ed.).

Bolton, Robert, *People Skills: How to Assert Yourself, Listen to Others, and Resolve Conflicts.* Englewood Cliffs, N.J.: Prentice-Hall, 1976.

Evered, James F., *Shirt Sleeves Management.* New York: AMACOM, 1981.

Herzberg, Frederick, *Work and the Nature of Man.* New York: John Wiley & Sons, 1966.

Lefton, Robert, Buzzotta, Vic, Sherberg, Manuel, and Karraker, Dean L., *Effective Motivation Through Performance Appraisal: Dimensional Appraisal Strategies.* Cambridge, Mass.: Ballinger Publishing Company/Harper & Row, 1980.

Lefton, Robert, Buzzotta, Vic, and Sherberg, Manuel, *Improving Productivity Through People Skills.* Cambridge, Mass.: Ballinger Publishing Company/Harper & Row, 1980.

Maslow, Abraham, "A Theory of Human Motivation." *Psychological Review* (1943), pp. 370–96.

Weiss, Donald H., *Getting Results: The Performance Appraisal Process.* New York: AMACOM, 1985.

————, *How to Manage for Higher Productivity.* New York: AMACOM, 1982.

————, *Managing Conflict.* New York: AMACOM, 1981.

Weiss, W. H., *Decision Making for First-Time Managers.* New York: AMACOM, 1985.

Index

About the Author

Donald H. Weiss is an Account Executive for Psychological Associates, a training and development company, and President of Self-Management Associates, a small-business consulting firm located in Dallas. Along with the six books in the Successful Office Skills series, he has written numerous books, articles, video scripts, and study guides on business management and related topics. Dr. Weiss is the author of AMACOM's popular cassette/workbook programs *Getting Results, How to Manage for Higher Productivity,* and *Managing Conflict.*

Dr. Weiss holds a Ph.D. in social theory from Tulane University, as well as degrees from the University of Arizona and the University of Missouri. He has also taught at several colleges and universities. He is a member of the American Society for Training and Development.